BELARUS 2016 HUMAN RIGHTS REPORT

EXECUTIVE SUMMARY

Belarus is an authoritarian state. The country's constitution provides for a directly elected president who is head of state, and a bicameral parliament, the national assembly. A prime minister appointed by the president is the nominal head of government, but power is concentrated in the presidency, both in fact and in law. Since his election as president in 1994, Aliaksandr Lukashenka has consolidated his rule over all institutions and undermined the rule of law through authoritarian means, including manipulated elections and arbitrary decrees. All subsequent presidential elections fell well short of international standards. The 2016 parliamentary elections also failed to meet international standards.

Civilian authorities, President Lukashenka in particular, maintained effective control over security forces.

The most significant human rights problems continued to be: citizens were unable to choose their government through elections; in a system bereft of checks and balances, authorities committed abuses; and former political prisoners' political rights remained largely restricted while the government failed to account for longstanding cases of politically motivated disappearances.

Other human rights problems included abuses by the security forces, which reportedly mistreated suspects during investigations and in prisons. Prison conditions remained poor. Authorities arbitrarily arrested, detained, and imprisoned citizens for criticizing officials, participating in demonstrations, and other political reasons. The judiciary experienced political interference and a lack of independence; trial outcomes often appeared predetermined, and trials occurred behind closed doors or in the absence of the accused. Authorities infringed on the right of privacy. The government restricted civil liberties, including freedom of speech, press, assembly, association, and religion. The government continued to hinder or prevent the activities of some religious groups, at times fining them or restricting their services. Official corruption in all branches of government remained a problem. Authorities harassed human rights groups, nongovernmental organizations (NGOs), and political parties, refusing to register many and then threatening them with criminal prosecution for operating without registration. Violence and discrimination against women were problems, as was violence against children. Trafficking in persons, including state-sponsored forced labor, remained a problem, although victim identification and protection slightly improved. There was discrimination against lesbian, gay, bisexual, transgender, and intersex (LGBTI) persons; those with disabilities; Roma and other ethnic minorities; persons with HIV/AIDS; and those who sought to use the Belarusian language. Authorities harassed and at times dismissed from their jobs members of independent unions in state-owned enterprises, severely limiting the ability of workers to form and join independent trade unions and to organize and bargain collectively. Authorities also employed various means of forced labor.

Authorities at all levels operated with impunity and failed to take steps to prosecute or punish officials in the government or security forces who committed human rights abuses.

Section 1. Respect for the Integrity of the Person, Including Freedom from:

a. Arbitrary Deprivation of Life and other Unlawful or Politically Motivated Killings

During the year there were no reports that the government or its agents committed arbitrary or unlawful killings and no reports of deaths from torture.

b. Disappearance

There were no developments in the reportedly continuing investigations into the 2000 disappearance of journalist Zmitser Zavadski and the 1999 disappearances of former deputy prime minister Viktar Hanchar, businessman Anatol Krasouski, and former interior minister Yuri Zakharanka. There was evidence of government involvement in the disappearances, but authorities continued to deny any connection with them.

In 2014 a senior Investigations Committee officer informed Zakharanka's mother that by law it was impossible to apply the statute of limitations in the case unless a suspect was identified and charged, and thus the case of her son could not be closed as she had requested. The committee also refused the mother's request to study case materials, citing that it was only possible upon completion of the preliminary investigation.

In May a Minsk court suspended the civil suit of Zakharanka's mother asking for the court to recognize Zakharanka's death until the criminal case about his disappearance was closed. The lawyer for Zakharanka's mother told the court, "given the fact that for 16 years the investigation has produced no results, it deprives the citizen the opportunity to realize her rights. In fact, it is a denial of justice."

On August 1, a Minsk city court refused the request of Zakharanka's mother to declare her son deceased. Zakharanka's mother repeatedly has asked the authorities to declare him dead and/or suspend the investigation, which would allow her access to the case materials and his property. In October authorities again extended the investigation into Zakharanka's disappearance until December 24.

c. Torture and Other Cruel, Inhuman, or Degrading Treatment or Punishment

The law prohibits such practices. Nevertheless, the Committee for State Security (KGB), riot police, and other security forces, often unidentified and in plain clothes, continued to beat detainees occasionally. Security forces also reportedly mistreated individuals during investigations. During arrests police occasionally beat criminal suspects and citizens.

Human rights advocates, opposition leaders, and activists released from detention facilities continued to report maltreatment and other forms of physical and psychological abuse of suspects during criminal and administrative investigations.

On January 12, various media reported that a Hrodna district court sentenced in closed hearings two senior police officers to four years and six years in jail, respectively, for "committing crimes related to violence, torture or abuse of suspects." Authorities also banned the two from holding any positions in law enforcement agencies for five years after their release from prison.

On January 25, during the opening of the trial in a Minsk district court of three individuals in the so-called graffiti case, authorities detained and then allegedly beat two youth activists, Paval Siarhei and Maksim Shytsik, after they unfolded a banner that read, "No to Political Persecution" and shouted, "Art is No Crime." Security officers removed the two activists from the courtroom. Paval Dabravolski, a journalist from the news portal *tut.by*, followed the activists and police from the courtroom. According to accounts from the activists and Dabravolski, police knocked the three to the ground, and punched and kicked them for some 20 minutes. Individuals standing outside the room could reportedly hear the assault. Security officers also removed all the footage from Dabravolski's media files. Police charged the three with resisting police orders, minor hooliganism, and contempt of court. Ultimately, the court fined the three. One of the unidentified officers who reportedly beat the three testified against them in court.

On February 19, Minister of Information Liliya Ananich claimed that Dabravolski had prevented police officers from performing their duties. The minister added that while the media law affords journalists certain rights, it also requires them to respect the rights and legitimate interests of other individuals and observe regulations. She referred to the Interior Ministry's claim that Dabravolski interfered with the police officers' conduct of their professional duties and was subsequently fined for that. The minister urged journalists to comply with the media law, the criminal code, and the norms of professional ethics.

On April 29, the Investigations Committee informed Dabravolski that it had denied his appeal to open a criminal investigation into alleged misuse of force by police officers against him and two opposition activists in the January 25th incident. The committee explained that the police officers' actions did not constitute elements of a crime and were aimed at "stopping Dabravolski's illegal actions." According to the committee, injuries inflicted on Dabravolski and the two activists and the traces of blood on their clothes "objectively fit" the policemen's testimony of their actions, and the committee's inquiry did not register any evidence of officers mistreating or using excessive force against the three individuals, who were not subjected "to brutal and inappropriate" treatment. The committee also accused Dabravolski of attacking an officer, refusing to identify himself as a journalist, illegally recording the detention of the two activists on a cell phone camera, and insulting police and threatening them with trouble at work by publishing defamatory information.

As in the previous year, observers reported a few isolated cases of new recruit hazing that included beatings and other forms of physical and psychological abuse. Observers believed there might have been fewer cases because of the government's increased prosecution of offenders. For example, on August 17, a district court in Brest sentenced a senior army servant to a 18 months of khimiya, a form of internal exile, for extorting money and personal belongings from new recruits, beating, and threatening to kill them. Authorities denied all appeals in this case in October.

Prison and Detention Center Conditions
Prison and detention center conditions remained poor and in many cases posed threats to life and health.

<u>Physical Conditions</u>: According to local activists and human rights lawyers, there were shortages of food, medicine, warm clothing, and bedding as well as inadequate access to basic or emergency medical care and clean drinking water. Ventilation in cells and overall sanitation were poor, and authorities failed to provide conditions necessary for maintaining proper personal hygiene. Prisoners frequently complained of malnutrition and low-quality uniforms and bedding. Some former political prisoners reported psychological abuse and sharing cells with violent criminals. The law permits family and friends to bring detainees food and hygiene products and to send them parcels by mail, but authorities did not always allow this.

Overcrowding of holding facilities and prisons continued to be a problem, although an amnesty, which began in June 2015, reduced the number of inmates. Ministry of Internal Affairs officials dismissed reports of overcrowding. Authorities allowed persons sentenced to a form of internal exile (khimiya) to work outside detention facilities; these individuals were required to return at night to prison barracks, where they lived under strict conditions and supervision.

Although there were isolated reports that police placed underage suspects in pretrial detention facility cells with adult suspects and convicts, authorities generally held juvenile prisoners separately from adults at juvenile penal colonies, arrest houses, and pretrial holding facilities. In general, conditions for female and juvenile prisoners were slightly better than for male prisoners.

According to human rights NGOs and former prisoners, authorities routinely abused prisoners. In cases of death of suspects or inmates resulting from alleged abuse or torture by prison officials, authorities continued to deny families of suspects or inmates a fair and transparent investigation and prosecution of reported incidents. After an outcry in independent media, for example, authorities in Zhodzina opened an investigation and a criminal case into the death from a reported heart failure of Ihar Barbaschynski, a 37-year-old retired army major, in a local jail on September 20. Barbaschynski's mother told the press that police originally arrested Ihar and his brother in Slutsk in March while they were walking home from a nightclub. Authorities reportedly accused the brothers of drinking in a public place. The following morning an ambulance took the two men from detention facilities to a hospital with multiple rib fractures and bruises, but they were neither charged nor detained in March. The brothers subsequently filed a complaint about police brutality to the local police department. In May police rearrested them on charges of allegedly using violence against police officers, and Barbaschynski remained in detention until his death in September.

On September 16, a Minsk district court started hearing a criminal case against a doctor, Aliaksandr Krylou, charged with negligence for the 2013 death of 21-year-old prisoner Ihar Ptichkin, who suffered a heart attack after an alleged beating. On October 21, the court sentenced Krylou to three years in jail. In the period 2013-16, Ptichkin's family filed numerous appeals to bring criminal charges against the prison's doctors, as well as to challenge multiple denials to investigate the case and bring it to prosecution.

Credible sources maintained that prison administrators employed inmates to intimidate political prisoners and compel confessions. They also reported that authorities neither explained nor protected political prisoners' legal rights and excessively penalized them for minor violations of the prison rules.

Given the poor medical care, observers believed tuberculosis, pneumonia, HIV/AIDS, and other communicable diseases were widespread in prisons. In 2014 a senior tuberculosis control officer reported that tuberculosis infection in prisons was quadruple the national average but claimed that only up to 4 percent of the 7,400 tuberculosis patients across the country were in prisons.

Human rights NGOs reported that prison inmates and individuals held in internal exile often complained of lack of employment opportunities or low pay. On August 18, the head of the Interior Ministry's Corrections Department, Siarhei Daroshka, stated that of the average 510-ruble ($205) salary, inmates would get only 10 percent and the rest would go to fund the costs of their imprisonment and to repay any debts or damages ordered by the court.

Administration: As in the previous year, authorities claimed to have conducted annual or more frequent investigations and monitoring of prison and detention center conditions. Human rights groups, however, asserted that such inspections, even if they did occur, lacked credibility given the absence of an ombudsman and the inability of reliable independent human rights advocates to visit prisons or provide consultations to prisoners.

Prisoners and detainees had limited access to visitors, and denial of meetings with families was a common punishment for disciplinary violations. Authorities often denied or delayed political prisoners' meetings with family as a means of pressure and intimidation.

Although the law provides for freedom of religion, and there were no reports of egregious infringements, authorities generally prevented prisoners from holding religious services and performing ceremonies that did not comply with prison regulations.

Former prisoners reported that prison officials often censored or did not forward their complaints to higher authorities and that prison administrators either ignored or selectively considered requests for investigation of alleged abuses. Prisoners also reported that prison administration frequently refused to provide them with copies of responses to their complaints, which further complicated their defense. Complaints could result in retaliation against prisoners who spoke out, including humiliation, death threats, or other forms of punishment and harassment.

Corruption in prisons was a serious problem, and observers noted that parole often depended on bribes to prison personnel or a prisoner's political affiliation.

Independent Monitoring: Despite numerous requests to the Ministries of Internal Affairs and Justice, government officials continued to refuse to meet with human rights advocates or approve requests from NGOs to visit detention and prison facilities. In its 2015 response to Paval Sapelka of the human rights NGO Vyasna, the Interior Ministry's Corrections Department claimed it would be "inexpedient" for him to visit detention facilities and monitor their conditions.

d. Arbitrary Arrest or Detention

The law limits arbitrary detention, but the government did not respect these limits. Authorities continued to arrest or detain individuals for political reasons and to use administrative measures to detain political activists before, during, and after protests and other major public events.

Role of the Police and Security Apparatus

The Ministry of Internal Affairs exercises authority over police, but other bodies outside of its control, for example, the KGB, the Financial Investigations Department of the State Control Committee, the Investigation Committee, and presidential security services exercise police functions. The president has the authority to subordinate all security bodies to his personal command. Impunity among law enforcement personnel remained a serious problem. Individuals have the right to report police abuse to a prosecutor, although the government often did not investigate reported abuses or hold perpetrators accountable.

Arrest Procedures and Treatment of Detainees

By law police must request permission from a prosecutor to detain a person for more than three hours, but police usually ignored this procedure and routinely detained and arrested individuals without warrants. Authorities may hold a criminal suspect for up to 10 days without filing formal charges and for up to 18 months after filing charges. Under the law prosecutors, investigators, and security service agencies have the authority to extend detention without consulting a judge. Detainees have the right to petition the court system regarding the legality of their detention, but authorities frequently suppressed or ignored such appeals.

Arbitrary Arrest: Authorities detained opposition and civil society activists for reasons widely considered politically motivated. In isolated cases, authorities used administrative measures to detain political activists before, during, and after planned demonstrations and protests, as well as other public events.

From January through March, scores of market vendors, opposition leaders, activists, and their supporters held unsanctioned demonstrations in Minsk to protest a presidential edict that banned the selling of clothing and footwear without certification of compliance with the Customs Union's safety requirements. While police did not interfere with the demonstrations, authorities routinely detained various regional activists en route to Minsk to prevent their participation in the demonstrations.

On September 11, the day of the parliamentary elections, authorities arrested Leanid Kulakou after the polls closed and on the next day sentenced him to three days in jail on minor hooliganism charges. Kulakou had monitored voting and tabulation on the day of the election.

Pretrial Detention: Authorities may hold a criminal suspect for up to 10 days without filing formal charges. Prior to being charged, the law provides detainees with no access to their families or to outside food and medical supplies, both of which are vital given poor conditions in detention facilities. Police routinely held persons for the full 10-day period before charging them.

Police often detained individuals for several hours, ostensibly to confirm their identity; fingerprinted them; and then released them without charge. Police and security forces frequently used this tactic to detain members of the democratic opposition and demonstrators, to prevent the distribution of leaflets and newspapers, or to break up civil society meetings and events. For example, on September 8, police detained four opposition activists, including Malady Front leader Zmitser Dashkevich, Volha Mikalaichyk, and Uladzimir Yaromenak, ahead of a planned protest in front of the Russian Embassy to mark the 502nd anniversary of the Battle of Orsha. Dashkevich was reportedly grabbed and beaten by plainclothes police officers in the courtyard of his apartment, while Mikalaichyk was forcefully detained when she approached the Russian embassy. Police released the four activists after several hours without filing charges.

Detainee's Ability to Challenge Lawfulness of Detention before a Court: Detainees have the right to petition the court system regarding the legality of their detention, but authorities frequently suppressed or ignored such appeals. By law courts have 24 hours to issue a ruling on a detention and 72 hours on an arrest. Courts hold closed hearings in these cases, which the suspect, a defense lawyer, and other legal representatives may attend. Prosecutors, suspects, and defense lawyers can appeal to higher courts the decision of the lower court within 24 hours of the ruling. Higher courts have three days to rule on appeals, and their rulings cannot be challenged. Further appeals can only be filed when investigators extend the period of detention.

e. Denial of Fair Public Trial

The constitution provides for an independent judiciary, but authorities did not respect judicial independence. Observers believed corruption, inefficiency, and political interference with judicial decisions were widespread. Courts convicted individuals on false and politically motivated charges brought by prosecutors, and observers believed that senior government leaders and local authorities dictated the outcomes of trials.

As in previous years, according to human rights groups, prosecutors wielded excessive and imbalanced authority because they may extend detention periods without the permission of judges. They also noted a power imbalance between the prosecution and the defense. Defense lawyers were unable to examine investigation files, be present during investigations and interrogations, or examine evidence against defendants until a prosecutor formally brought the case to court. Lawyers found it difficult to challenge some evidence because the Prosecutor's Office controlled all technical expertise. According to many defense attorneys, this power imbalance persisted throughout the year, especially in politically motivated criminal and administrative cases. Courts did not exonerate criminal defendants except in rare circumstances during the year.

By law bar associations are independent, and licensed lawyers are permitted to establish private practices or bureaus. All lawyers, however, must be licensed by the Ministry of Justice and must renew their licenses every five years.

In the past the justice ministry used disbarment as a tool in political cases; the ministry accused the disbarred lawyers of distorting information about the investigations of their clients, their state of health, and their conditions of detention. During the year there were no new disbarments, but no disbarred lawyers had their licenses restored.

Trial Procedures

The law provides for the presumption of innocence. Nevertheless, the lack of judicial independence, the state media practice of reporting on high-profile cases as if guilt were already certain, and widespread limits on defense rights frequently placed the burden of proving innocence on the defendant.

The law also provides for public trials, but authorities occasionally closed trials and frequently held them in judges' offices, where attendance was limited. Judges adjudicate all trials. For the most serious cases, two civilian advisers assist the judge.

The law provides defendants the right to attend proceedings, confront witnesses, and present evidence on their own behalf, but authorities did not always respect these rights.

The law provides for access to legal counsel for detainees and requires that courts appoint a lawyer for those who cannot afford one. Although by law defendants can ask for their trials to be conducted in Belarusian, most judges and prosecutors were not fluent in Belarusian, rejected motions for interpreters, and proceeded in Russian. The law provides for the right to choose legal representation freely; however, a presidential decree prohibits NGO members who are lawyers from representing individuals other than members of their organizations in court. The government's disbarment of attorneys who represented political opponents of the regime further limited defendants' choice of counsel. The government also required defense attorneys to sign non-disclosure statements that limited their ability to release any information about the case to the public, media, and even defendants' family members.

Courts often allowed statements obtained by force and threats of bodily harm during interrogations to be used against defendants. Some defendants were tried in absentia. For example, on January 19, a district court in Minsk fined in absentia Paval Sevyarynets, co-chair of the unregistered Belarusian Christian Democracy Party, 525 rubles ($250) for participating in an unsanctioned demonstration in November 2015. During the demonstration, up to 110 individuals marched from a department store to the Central Election Committee's building in Minsk to mark the 1996 referendum that stripped the powers of the parliament and expanded the powers of the president.

Defendants have the right to appeal convictions, and most defendants did so. Nevertheless, appeals courts upheld the verdicts of the lower courts in the vast majority of cases.

Political Prisoners and Detainees

Local human rights organizations reported several different lists of political prisoners in the country. These included individuals who were facing criminal charges and others who were already incarcerated. Leading local human rights groups, including Vyasna and the Belarusian Helsinki Committee, either recognized these individuals as prisoners of conscience or noted serious due process violations that they suggested required, at the very least, a retrial.

On October 12, for example, a Minsk district court convicted Dzmitry Palienka, an opposition and anarchist movement activist and participant of the "Critical Mass" ride on April 29, of using violence against a traffic police officer during his detention and of distributing pornographic images in social media. The judge sentenced Palienka to a two-year-suspended sentence, as well as forced rehabilitation for alcoholism. The activist was released in court. Human rights advocates welcomed the "government's restraint" in not imprisoning Palienka but recognized him as a political prisoner when he was in pretrial detention.

Eduard Palchys, blogger and editor of the 1863x.com website, was detained in January and charged in June with inciting racial, ethnic, or religious hatred and producing and distributing pornographic materials. The prosecution against Palchys focused on nine articles published on his website that were highly critical of Russia and the "Russkiy Mir" concept. Palchys was also accused of distributing pornographic materials for reposting a Russian-website's post critical of Belarusian culture and independence, which included a photo of a nude woman. Palchys claimed the post was to demonstrate the amount of anti-Belarusian sentiment in Russia and was not meant to be seen as pornography. His trial was closed to the press and observers. Several domestic human rights groups recognized Palchys as a political prisoner on October 5. On October 28, Palchys was found guilty of inciting racial, ethnic, or religious hatred and distributing pornographic materials, but he was given a suspended 21-month sentence and was subject to a travel ban. Prior to his trial, some human rights groups recognized him as a political prisoner. Human rights groups welcomed his release but noted that the government continued to restrict the freedom of speech.

On August 10, human rights advocates, including the human rights center Vyasna and the Belarusian Helsinki Committee, recognized Uladzimir Kondrus as a political prisoner. Authorities arrested Kondrus on June 14 and charged him under the Criminal Code's provision dealing with mass protests, which has a 10-year statute of limitations. Kondrus was alleged to have been involved in the postelection demonstrations in December 2010, when he was allegedly seen holding a large piece of wood and breaking windows at the parliament building, as well as attacking riot police officers during the protests. Human rights groups called for his immediate release and the suspension of the criminal prosecution against him, claiming that his actions in 2010 could only qualify as hooliganism, which carries a five-year statute of limitations, and not as a violation of the Criminal Code's prohibition on mass protests, which has a 10-year statute of limitations. On November 16, the first day of his trial, Kondrus purported to attempt to slit his writs, and the judge ordered him to undergo a psychiatric assessment. On December 26, the court sentenced Kondrus to 18 months of "restricted freedom"; he was released from detention following the hearing. The psychiatric assessment reportedly alleged that Kondrus had a psychiatric condition, and the court ordered him to undergo mandatory psychiatric treatment during his period of restricted freedom.

In August 2015 President Lukashenka released six individuals considered political prisoners by human rights organizations, including 2010 presidential candidate Mikalai Statkevich.

During their court hearings, defendants in politically motivated cases reported threats against associates and family members to compel testimony against the defendants, as well as pressure to sign confessions.

Prison authorities often confiscated and censored mail of political prisoners, reportedly to exert pressure by further isolating prisoners and limiting their contacts with families and associates.

Former political prisoners who had been pardoned continued to be unable to exercise some civil and political rights at year's end. For example, on July 9, the Central Electoral Commission refused to register the initiative group supporting the candidacy for parliament of former political prisoner and 2010 presidential candidate Mikalai Statkevich because any individual in prison or with a criminal record is prohibited by law from being a candidate.

Authorities removed restrictions against several prominent former political prisoners. For example, on February 4, police in Vaukavysk lifted preventive supervision limitations against anticorruption activist Mikalai Autukhovich, who previously was not permitted to travel outside the city without official permission. In a separate case, on March 9, investigators dropped all criminal charges and a subsequent travel ban against former presidential candidate Ales Mikhalevich in connection with 2010 postelection demonstrations.

Civil Judicial Procedures and Remedies

The law provides that individuals can file lawsuits seeking damages for a human rights violation, but the civil judiciary was not independent and was rarely impartial in such matters.

f. Arbitrary or Unlawful Interference with Privacy, Family, Home, or Correspondence

The law prohibits such actions, but the government did not respect these prohibitions. Authorities used wiretapping, video surveillance, and a network of informers that deprived persons of privacy.

By law persons who obstruct law enforcement personnel in the performance of their duties can be penalized or charged with an administrative offense, even if the "duties" are inconsistent with the law. "Obstruction" could include any effort to prevent KGB or law enforcement officers from entering the premises of a company, establishment, or organization; refusing to allow KGB audits; or denying or restricting KGB access to information systems and databases.

The law requires a warrant before, or immediately after, conducting a search. Nevertheless, some democratic activists believed the KGB entered their homes unannounced. The KGB has the authority to enter any building at any time, as long as it applies for a warrant within 24 hours after the entry.

Security forces continued to target prominent opposition and civil society leaders with arbitrary searches and interrogations at border crossings and airports. For example, on September 8, border officials detained co-chairman of the Belarusian Christian Democracy Party Vital Rymasheuski and leader of the United Civic Party Anatol Lyabedzka for about an hour at the Belarus-Lithuania border. The two were on their way to a conference in Vilnius, and the border guards seized several dozen election campaign leaflets that Lyabedzka had with him, but eventually authorities let the two proceed and apologized for the delay.

On November 8, customs officers confiscated five copies of a book authored by Andrei Sannikau, 2010 presidential candidate and former political prisoner who lives in the United Kingdom, from his spouse and prominent journalist Iryna Khalip. She was returning to Belarus from Poland with their son and carrying copies of the book *My Story: Belarusian Amerikanka or Elections Under Dictatorship* inscribed by the author to various friends and supporters. Officials told her the books would be examined by experts for at least a month before they could be returned to her. The book tells the story of Sannikau's arrest for participating in the December 2010 postelection demonstration in Minsk, his experiences in prison, his release in 2012, as well as international media coverage of his imprisonment.

While the law prohibits authorities from intercepting telephone and other communications without a prosecutor's order, authorities routinely monitored residences, telephones, and computers. Nearly all opposition political figures and many prominent members of civil society groups claimed that authorities monitored their conversations and activities. The government continued to collect and obtain personally identifiable information on independent journalists and democratic activists during raids and by confiscating computer equipment.

The law allows the KGB, the Ministry of Internal Affairs, special security services, financial intelligence personnel, and certain border guard detachments to use wiretaps. Wiretaps require the permission of a prosecutor, but the lack of prosecutorial independence rendered this requirement meaningless.

The Ministry of Communications has the authority to terminate the telephone service of persons who violate their telephone contracts, which prohibit the use of telephone services for purposes contrary to state interests and public order. Cell phone providers are banned from selling cell phone cards to customers who do not produce their passports or to foreigners who are not registered with local immigration services.

Authorities continued to harass family members of NGO leaders and civil society and opposition activists through selective application of the law.

Section 2. Respect for Civil Liberties, Including:

a. Freedom of Speech and Press

The constitution provides for freedom of speech and the press. The government did not respect these rights and enforced numerous laws to control and censor the public and the media. Moreover, the state press propagated views in support of President Lukashenka and official policies, without giving room for critical voices.

Freedom of Speech and Expression: Individuals could not criticize President Lukashenka and the government publicly or discuss matters of general public interest without fear of reprisal. Authorities videotaped political meetings, conducted frequent identity checks, and used other forms of intimidation. Authorities also prohibited wearing facemasks, displaying unregistered or opposition flags and symbols, and displaying placards bearing messages deemed threatening to the government or public order.

On January 29, a Minsk district court fined three men, Maksim Pekarski, Viachaslau Kasinerau, and Vadzim Zheromski, in the so-called graffiti case; the fines ranged from 630 rubles ($300) to 1,050 rubles ($500) on the charges of property damage. While the judge dropped the criminal charges of hooliganism and vandalism, the three were convicted of painting graffiti with patriotic slogans, such as, "Belarus should be Belarusian," that police deemed to be "promoting violence in society and disregard of universally accepted rules of conduct." Police brutally detained the three men and their two associates, who were later released without charge, in August 2015, and Kasinerau told the press in September 2015 that during his detention, police bundled him into a bus, and an officer hit him in the face, fracturing his jaw. When they arrived at the police precinct, investigators pressured him to plead guilty and showed him records of his private phone conversations with his spouse, which were reportedly wiretapped months before the arrest. Although authorities opened an investigation into his reported beating, there were no developments during the year in bringing any charges related to police brutality.

The law also limits free speech by criminalizing actions such as giving information to a foreigner about the political, economic, social, military, or international situation of the country that authorities deem false or derogatory.

Press and Media Freedoms: Government restrictions limited access to information and often resulted in media self-censorship. State-controlled media did not provide balanced coverage and overwhelmingly presented the official version of events. Appearances by opposition politicians on state media were limited, primarily to those required by law during election campaigns. Authorities warned, fined, detained, and interrogated members of media.

Under the law, the government may close a publication, printed or online, after two warnings in one year for violating a range of restrictions on the press. Additionally, regulations give authorities arbitrary power to prohibit or censor reporting. The Information Ministry can suspend periodicals or newspapers for three months without a court ruling. The law also prohibits the media from disseminating information on behalf of unregistered political parties, trade unions, and NGOs.

On March 2, the Information Ministry announced that it issued warnings to two independent, internet publications: the online newspaper *Yezhednevnik* and the online version of the print newspaper *Nasha Niva*. The former purportedly violated the media law by using images of World War II German military equipment in an article about the armed forces' readiness checks, which, according to the ministry "discredited the army." *Nasha Niva* was warned for violating the law by publishing an article about the demographic situation in the country, which reportedly did not comply with figures released by the National Statistics Committee, and discredited the "successful" demographic policies of the government. The independent Belarusian Association of Journalists condemned the warnings as far-fetched penalties, violations of media freedom, and an unacceptable measure to censor publications.

Limited information was available in the state-run press about the September parliamentary election, including about independent candidates. Although authorities did not generally censor the publication of candidates' programs in print media, some opposition candidates complained that local television channels refused to televise their addresses. For example, in Hrodna Mikalai Ulasevich, a United Civic Party member and antinuclear activist, accused authorities of not broadcasting his speech, which included criticism of the country's nuclear power plant project and discussion of corruption and lack of local governance. In another case, Siarhei Kalyakin, leader of the Just World Belarusian Party of the Left, complained to the regional election commission that the text of his biography was edited without his authorization on the official poster listing the biographies of all candidates in the Orsha district. The printed text of Kalyakin's biography was missing a sentence referring to Kalyakin's efforts as an MP to impeach President Lukashenka in 1996. State media otherwise provided only limited coverage of the campaign, focusing largely on the activities of the president and other state officials as well as political statements of the Central Election Commission chairperson.

On February 7, Information Minister Liliya Ananich warned media about criticizing the government and against publicizing inaccurate information, in particular taking remarks or statements out of a broader context, and fomenting negative sentiments, which she described as "destructive." She committed to continue tight monitoring of the internet and printed media, so "they serve [the cause of] consolidation of society." Ananich stated that any media violating the country's laws would receive official warnings and subsequently be blocked.

The Information Ministry continued to deny registration to independent media outlets. In spite of the lack of registration, independent media, including newspapers, magazines, and internet news websites, sought to provide coverage of events. They operated, however, under repressive media laws, and most faced discriminatory publishing and distribution policies, including limiting access to government officials and press briefings, controlling the size of press runs of papers, and raising the cost of printing.

State-owned media dominated the information field and maintained the highest circulation through generous subsidies and preferences. There was no countrywide private television. The state-owned postal system, Belposhta, and the state-owned kiosk system, Belsayuzdruk, continued to refuse to deliver or sell numerous independent newspapers that covered politics. For example, on September 14, Aksana Kolb, an editor of the *Novy Chas* independent weekly newspaper, told the press that Belposhta and Belsayuzdruk had refused to distribute the newspaper through their subscription and retail chains, respectively. *Novy Chas* is a Belarusian-language weekly that publishes materials about national culture, history, identity, and information related to reinforcing the country's sovereignty.

The exclusion of the independent printed press from the state distribution system and the requirement that private stores secure registration to sell printed media effectively limited the ability of the independent press to distribute their publications.

Although authorities continued to allow the circulation of *Narodnaya Volya* and *Nasha Niva*, two independent national newspapers, through state distribution systems, they remained subject to restrictions on the number of copies allowed to circulate.

Several independent newspapers, including *Vitsyebski Kuryer*, *Salidarnasc*, *BDG*, and *Bobruysky Kuryer*, disseminated internet-only versions due to printing and distribution restrictions.

International media continued to operate in the country but not without interference and prior censorship. Euronews and the Russian channels First Channel, NTV, and RTR were generally available, although only through paid cable services in many parts of the country and then with a lag time that allowed the removal of news deemed undesirable by authorities. At times authorities blocked, censored, or replaced their international news programs with local programming.

<u>Violence and Harassment</u>: Authorities continued to harass and detain local and foreign journalists routinely.

Security forces continually hampered efforts of independent journalists to cover demonstrations and protests in Minsk and across the country. The independent Belarusian Association of Journalists reported that, as of November 11, police detained at least six journalists while performing their professional duties.

The government routinely denied accreditation to journalists who work with foreign media. As of November 1, at least two journalists had been fined in 10 cases for not having government accreditation or cooperating with a foreign media outlet.

Agnieszka Romaszewska-Guzy, director of the Warsaw-based Belarusian-language channel *Belsat,* told media on June 1 that the Ministry of Foreign Affairs did not respond to its application to accredit 10 local journalists. The ministry was supposed to respond to the accreditation application by May 21. She pledged that the unregistered Minsk-based office and journalists across the country would continue their operations and would "not adjust our reporting to meet the Belarusian authorities' wishes because we represent free journalism."

Independent journalist and military expert Aliaksandr Alesin was detained in November 2014 and faced charges of cooperating with foreign intelligence sources, which carry a maximum penalty of two years' imprisonment. He was released in December 2014, although he was banned from leaving the country. On January 20, he told the press that authorities suspended the criminal charges brought against him for allegedly "establishing cooperation on a confidential basis with a foreign security or intelligence service."

<u>Censorship or Content Restrictions</u>: The government exerted pressure on the vast majority of independent publications to exercise self-censorship, warning them not to report on certain topics or criticize the government. The government tightly and directly controlled the content of state broadcast and print media. Local independent television stations operated in some areas and reported local news, although most were under government pressure to forgo reporting on national and sensitive issues or risk censorship.

Authorities allowed only state-run radio and television networks to broadcast nationwide. The government used this national monopoly to disseminate its version of events and minimize alternative or opposing viewpoints. Authorities banned state media from citing works and broadcasting music by independent local and well-known foreign musicians, artists, writers, and painters who were named on an alleged, unofficial nationwide blacklist for speaking in support of political prisoners and opposition or democratic activists.

Authorities warned businesses not to advertise in newspapers that criticized the government. As a result, independent media outlets operated under severe budgetary constraints.

Journalists reporting for international media that gave extensive coverage to the country, such as the Warsaw-based independent satellite channel Belsat TV and Radio Racyja, were denied press accreditation and received warnings from the Prosecutor's Office and heavy fines.

<u>Libel/Slander Laws</u>: Libel is a criminal offense. There are large fines and prison sentences of up to four years for defaming or insulting the president. Penalties for defamation of character make no distinction between private and public persons.

A public figure who is criticized for poor performance while in office may sue both the journalist and the media outlet that disseminated the critical report.

On September 23, a Minsk city court declined an appeal in the case of Aliaksandr Lapitski, who was convicted on April 12 of "committing socially dangerous acts" and violating Article 368 ("insulting the President of the Republic of Belarus"), Article 369 ("insulting the authorities"), Article 391 ("insulting a judge or a lay judge") of the Criminal Code of Belarus. The charges against Lapitski stem from e-mails and blog posts he wrote that, according to the authorities, insulted the president. Authorities alleged that Lapitski suffered from mental illness and sentenced him to a period of compulsory psychiatric treatment. Human rights group Vyasna called on authorities to end prosecution for defamation offenses and claimed that Lapitski's involuntary hospitalization infringed on his personal freedom.

<u>National Security</u>: Authorities frequently cited national security as grounds for censorship of media.

Internet Freedom

The government interfered with internet freedom by reportedly monitoring e-mail and internet chat rooms. While individuals, groups, and publications were generally able to engage in the peaceful expression of views via the internet, including by e-mail, all who did so risked possible legal and personal repercussions, and at times were believed to practice self-censorship. Opposition activists' e-mails and other web-based communications were likely to be monitored.

In January 2015 authorities introduced media law amendments making news websites and any internet information sources subject to the same regulations as print media. Under the amended law, online news providers must remove content and publish corrections if ordered to do so by the authorities and must adhere to a prohibition against "extremist" information. Amendments also restricted access to websites whose content includes promotion of violence, wars, "extremist activities"; materials related to illicit weapons, explosives, and drugs; trafficking in persons; pornography; and information that can harm the national interests of the country. Authorities may block access to sites that fail to obey government orders, including because of a single violation of distributing prohibited information, without a prosecutor or court's mandate. In addition, owners of internet sites may be held liable for users' comments that carry any prohibited information, and these sites may be blocked. The amended law also mandates the creation of a database of news websites. If a news website receives two or more formal warnings from the authorities, it may be removed from the database and lose its right to distribute information. Amendments also prohibit foreign states and foreign individuals from holding more than a 20 percent stake in local media companies.

While the list of blocked internet resources remained unavailable to the public, from January 2015 to March 2016 the Ministry of Information reportedly blocked access to 46 internet sites for drug trafficking, for distributing extremist materials, for illicit promotion of medications, for child pornography or for other content violations. Independent online media outlets were not generally blocked during the year, however, the election monitoring mission of the Organization for Security and Co-operation in Europe's Office for Democratic Institutions and Human Rights (OSCE/ODIHR) stated in a postelection press conference that its observers monitoring online news noted at least four online news sources, including popular news portal *tut.by,* had unexplained outages on election day, September 11.

The authorities reportedly monitored internet traffic. By law the telecommunications monopoly, Beltelekam, and other organizations authorized by the government have the exclusive right to maintain internet domains.

A presidential edict requires registration of service providers and internet websites, and requires the collection of information on users at internet cafes. It requires service providers to store data on individuals' internet use for a year and provide that information to law enforcement agencies upon request. Violations of the edict are punishable by prison sentences.

State companies and organizations, which included the workplaces of up to 70 percent of the country's workers, reportedly had internet filters.

In response to the government's interference and internet restrictions, many opposition groups and independent newspapers switched to internet domains operating outside the country. Observers said the few remaining independent media sites with domestic ".BY" (Belarus) domain suffixes practiced self-censorship at times.

On several occasions, cyberattacks of unknown origin temporarily disabled independent news portals and social networking sites.

According to various media sources, the number of internet users reached more than seven million persons, of which approximately 90 percent used the internet daily or numerous times a month. Internet penetration was approximately 83 percent among users 15 to 50 years of age.

Academic Freedom and Cultural Events

The government restricted academic freedom and cultural events.

Educational institutions were required to teach an official state ideology that combined reverence for the achievements of the former Soviet Union and of Belarus under the leadership of Lukashenka. Government-mandated textbooks contained a heavily propagandized version of history and other subjects. Authorities obligated all schools, including private institutions, to follow state directives to inculcate the official ideology and prohibited schools from being led by opposition members. The education minister has the right to appoint and dismiss the heads of private educational institutions.

Use of the word "academic" was restricted, and NGOs were prohibited from including the word "academy" in their titles. Opportunities to receive a higher education in the Belarusian language (vice Russian) in the majority of fields of study were scarce. The administrations of higher educational institutions made no effort to accommodate students wishing to study in Belarusian-language classes.

The Belarusian Republican Youth Union (BRYU), an official organization modeled on the Soviet-era KOMSOMOL, urged university students to join the BRYU to receive benefits and dormitory rooms. Local authorities also pressured BRYU members to campaign on behalf of government parliamentary candidates and to vote early. Students from various universities and colleges reported to an independent election-monitoring group that their faculties were pressuring students into early voting by threatening them with eviction from their dormitories. Additionally, authorities at times reportedly pressured students to act as informants for the country's security services.

According to an Education Ministry directive, educational institutions may expel students who engage in anti-government or unsanctioned political activity and must ensure the proper ideological education of students. School officials, however, cited poor academic performance or absence from classes as the official reason for expulsions. On January 20, Hleb Vaykul, a second-year student of the philology department, received final orders of his expulsion from the Belarusian

State University. Earlier in January Vaykul announced he had been expelled, at which time the university stated the expulsion orders had not been signed. The student called his expulsion politically motivated as he was one of the organizers of a December 2015 student protest against the university's decision to impose fees to retake exams. Authorities fined Vaykul 324 rubles ($175) for organizing through the "Students Against" community on the social networking website VKontakte and participating in the unsanctioned demonstration. The university administration stated Vaykul was expelled for failing to pass an examination on the psychology of literary works three times and not attending classes for the course during the fall semester.

The government continued to discourage and prevent teachers and activists from advancing the wider use of the Belarusian language and the preservation of Belarusian culture. A number of universities across the country continued not to enroll students in their undergraduate Belarusian linguistic programs for teachers of the Belarusian language and literature, citing low demand and a low number of applications in recent years.

The government also restricted cultural events, selectively approving performances of what they deemed opposition music groups at small concert halls. Approvals required groups to go through cumbersome and time-consuming procedures to receive permissions. The procedures continued to force some opposition theater and music groups out of public venues and into bars and private apartments by banning their performances.

Organizers of Theater Ch, an independent theater troupe, announced on January 20 that their two scheduled performances at the Modern Arts Center in Minsk were cancelled with short notice by the center's administration. Opposition leaders, 2010 presidential candidates, and former political prisoners Uladzimir Nyaklyaeu and Mikalai Statkevich attended the premier of their play *What to do with the Tiger?* and took pictures with the cast after the performance. The administration of the Modern Arts Center claimed they cancelled the performances after only four tickets were sold, while Theater Ch's managers reported that the two shows in January were sold out. The Polish Institute in Minsk sponsored the production of the play.

The government also restricted the activities of a nonofficial writers union, the independent Union of Belarusian Writers, and extensively supported the progovernment Union of Writers of Belarus. Authorities harassed distributors of books authored by critical and independent writers or written in the Belarusian language. Although sold at bookstores and online across the country, authorities did not allow printing houses and publishers to print copies of books by Sviatlana Aleksievich, winner of the Nobel prize for literature.

b. Freedom of Peaceful Assembly and Association

Freedom of Assembly

The constitution provides for freedom of peaceful assembly; however, the government severely restricted this right. Authorities employed a variety of means to discourage demonstrations, disperse them, minimize their effect, and punish the participants.

Only registered political parties, trade unions, and NGOs could request permission to hold a demonstration of more than 1,000 persons. Authorities usually denied requests by independent and opposition groups. A general atmosphere of repression and the threat of imprisonment or large fines exercised a chilling effect on potential protest organizers. This appeared to have resulted in fewer and smaller demonstrations.

The law criminalizes the announcement of demonstrations via the internet or social media before official approval, the participation in the activities of unregistered NGOs, the training of persons to demonstrate, the financing of public demonstrations, or the solicitation of foreign assistance "to the detriment" of the country. Violations are punishable by up to three years in prison.

Organizers must apply at least 15 days in advance for permission to conduct a public demonstration, rally, or meeting, and government officials are required to respond no later than five days prior to the scheduled event. Authorities, however, generally granted permits only for opposition demonstrations if held far from city centers. Authorities used intimidation and threats to discourage persons from participating in demonstrations, openly videotaped participants, and imposed heavy fines or jail sentences on participants in unsanctioned demonstrations. In addition, authorities required organizers to conclude contracts with police, fire department, health, and sanitary authorities for their services during and after a mass event. In some localities, local officials told permit applicants that they must first secure these contracts before a permit could be issued. When the applicants asked the police, fire department, health, and sanitary authorities to sign contracts, however, they were told they first must have an approved permit. Any individual found guilty of violating the law on mass events may not apply for another permit for a year following the conviction. From January through March, local authorities across the country rejected a number of applications for permission for market vendors to stage small demonstrations to protest new regulations that ban vendors from selling clothing and footwear without documents certifying their compliance with the Customs Union's safety requirements.

Opposition activists held dozens of unsanctioned rallies during the year and faced administrative charges and fines for allegedly violating the Law on Mass Events. Those who refused to pay fines, calling them politically motivated, potentially faced property confiscation and travel bans. Authorities regularly fined the same activists for their continuous political activity during the year. For example, on March 24, a Minsk district court fined approximately 11 opposition leaders and activists for participating in an unsanctioned February 28 demonstration in Minsk. Mikalai Statkevich, 2010 presidential candidate and former political prisoner, European Belarus campaign activist Maksim Vinyarski, and independent filmmaker Volha Mikalaichyk were tried in absentia and fined 105 rubles ($520) each. The court imposed similar fines on United Civic Party leader Anatol Lyabedzka and member Mikalai Kazlou, Belarusian Christian Democracy co-chair Vital Rymasheuski, market vendor Ales Makayeu, and European Belarus campaign activist Leanid Kulakou. Mikalai Autukhovich, a businessman from Vaukavysk and former political prisoner, and opposition activist Mikalai Kolas were fined 420 rubles ($210) each.

Authorities took various measures to limit how prodemocracy activists celebrated Freedom Day, the March 25 anniversary of the country's 1918 declaration of independence (an event the government does not recognize), although Minsk city authorities authorized a demonstration. In the permit issued by Minsk authorities, the route requested by activists from central Minsk was changed to a remote park. While approximately 2,000 opposition and civil society activists participated in the sanctioned rally, approximately 600 defied the permit by marching to the central part of Minsk, laying flowers at the Yanka Kupala monument, and holding a demonstration with political speeches at the monument. For their activities during the unsanctioned-route march, authorities fined a number of activists. opposition leaders Paval Sevyarynets, Uladzimir Nyaklyaeu, Mikalai Statkevich, Anatol Lyabedzka, and several activists, including Leanid Kulakou, Maksim Vinyarski, Zmitser Dashkevich, and others received fines for their activities on March 25.

In spite of providing a permit to the opposition to demonstrate, authorities also fined a number of opposition leaders and activists for participating in the sanctioned rally and speaking at the assembly point of the March 25 sanctioned demonstration. Police alleged that activists, who addressed the crowd at the gathering point, violated the permit, which allowed participants to gather but not demonstrate at the assembly point and speak only at the venue of the actual demonstration at a remote park. For example, Ryhor Kastuseu, a Belarusian Popular Front deputy chair, told the press that he received a notice that on May 5 a district court fined him in absentia 630 rubles ($320) also for violating the Law on Mass Events, when he spoke at the assembly point of the March 25 Freedom Day sanctioned demonstration. Though Kastuseu was only at locations sanctioned by the city authorities, police claimed that since he spoke at the gathering point, it violated the permit.

On May 16, a court in Maladzechna convicted activist Paval Siarhei for holding an unsanctioned rally in front of the local government building on May 12 and sentenced him to seven days in jail. He was detained on May 14 and was kept in holding facilities pending trial. Siarhei and other activists protested the continuing construction of two large hog farms near the city on May 12.

Freedom of Association

The law provides for freedom of association, but the government restricted it and selectively enforced laws and registration regulations to restrict the operation of independent associations that might criticize the government. Particularly since 2010, authorities have sought to close any legal loopholes they considered beneficial to NGOs.

All NGOs, political parties, and trade unions must receive Ministry of Justice approval to become registered. A government commission reviews and approves all registration applications; it based its decisions largely on political and ideological compatibility with official views and practices.

Actual registration procedures required applicants to provide the number and names of founders, along with a physical address in a nonresidential building for an office, an extraordinary burden in view of the tight financial straits of most NGOs, and individual property owners' fears of renting space to independent groups. Individuals listed as members were vulnerable to reprisal. The government's refusal to rent office space to unregistered organizations and the expense of renting private space reportedly forced most organizations to use residential addresses, which authorities could use as a reason to deny registration or to deregister. The law criminalizes activities conducted on behalf of unregistered groups and subjects group members to penalties ranging from large fines to two years in prison (also see section 7.a.).

Following the 2010 repression, authorities sought to close any legal loopholes they considered beneficial to NGOs. For example, the law on public associations prohibits NGOs from keeping funds for local activities at foreign financial institutions. The law also prohibits NGOs from facilitating provision of any support or benefits from foreign states to civil servants based on their political or religious views or ethnicity, a provision widely believed to be aimed at the Polish minority.

Only registered NGOs can legally accept foreign grants and technical aid and only for a limited set of approved activities. NGOs must receive approval from the Department for Humanitarian Affairs of the Presidential Administration and the Ministry of the Economy for technical aid before they can accept such funds or register the grants.

The government continued to deny registration to NGOs and political parties, which President Lukashenka frequently labeled as "the fifth column," on a variety of pretexts, including "technical" problems with applications. Authorities frequently harassed and intimidated individuals who identified themselves as founding members of organizations in an effort to induce them to abandon their membership and thus deprive groups of the number of petitioners necessary for registration. Many of the rejected groups previously had been denied registration on multiple occasions.

On January 5, authorities in Hrodna refused to register an NGO called Mothers' Movement 328, consisting of a group of mothers and wives who seek to defend the rights of their children and spouses, who were convicted under Article 328 of the Criminal Code for illegal drug trafficking and who, according to their families, received incommensurately long prison sentences. Larysa Zhygar, the leader of the NGO, said that authorities noted questions about the name of the group and its stated goals, which included charitable activities and assisting former prisoners and drug addicts, in their decision to reject the NGO's application for registration.

The Supreme Court upheld the Justice Ministry's decisions to deny registration to the Christian Democratic Movement, a nascent NGO affiliated with the unregistered Belarusian Christian Democracy party, and the Campaign for Fair Elections. On March 10, the Court denied an appeal filed by the campaign on the grounds that a letter of guarantee from an individual providing the organization with an office had not been notarized and that the banker's order contained abbreviations. This was the campaign's fourth registration denial. Separately, on March 14, the court also turned down an appeal from the Christian Movement to challenge the Justice Ministry's denial, citing the lack of an office number in the organization's legal address, among other grounds as a reason for the denial.

On April 18, the Supreme Court dismissed an appeal from the Belarusian Christian Democracy Party to challenge the Justice Ministry's March 3 decision not to register the party, citing "gross violations" of procedures to establish a party. According to the ministry's press release, a number of individuals, who were stated as founders of the party on the registration application, denied any connection to the party and claimed they did not participate in the party's founding convention after they were reportedly pressured to withdraw and threatened to be dismissed from jobs or expelled from universities. Additionally, "certain individuals on the founders' list were duplicated, and some of the personal information listed for founders was not valid," the ministry explained. The ministry also claimed that some of the founders the party listed on its application were not citizens of Belarus This was the sixth time that the party has been denied registration.

On July 31, a show on the main state television channel, Belarus1, claimed that the Vilnius-registered Independent Institute for Social, Economic, and Political Studies (IISEPS) did not actually conduct polls in the country, but rather it put together falsified data. IISEPS announced on August 9 that it would suspend all polling in the country due to "authorities destroying the polling network."

c. Freedom of Religion

See the Department of State's *International Religious Freedom Report* at www.state.gov/religiousfreedomreport/.

d. Freedom of Movement, Internally Displaced Persons, Protection of Refugees, and Stateless Persons

The law provides for freedom of movement, including the right to emigrate, but the government at times restricted the right of citizens, former political prisoners in particular to foreign travel. The government cooperated with the Office of the UN High Commissioner for Refugees (UNHCR) and other humanitarian organizations to provide protection and assistance to internally displaced persons, refugees, returning refugees, asylum seekers, stateless persons, and other persons of concern.

<u>In-country Movement</u>: Passports serve as a form of identity and authorities required them for permanent housing, work, and hotel registration. Police continued to harass selectively individuals who lived at a location other than their legal place of residence indicated in mandatory stamps in their passports.

The law also requires persons who travel to areas within 15 miles of the border (aside from authorized crossing points) to obtain an entrance pass.

<u>Foreign Travel</u>: The government's database of persons banned from traveling abroad contained the names of individuals who possessed state secrets, faced criminal prosecution or civil suits, or had outstanding financial obligations. Authorities informed some persons by letter that their names were in the database; others learned only at border crossings. The Internal Affairs Ministry and security agencies, border and customs services, and financial investigation departments have a right to place persons on "preventive" surveillance lists.

Students required permission from the head of their educational institution to study abroad. Ostensibly intended to counter trafficking in persons, the Ministry of Internal Affairs is also required to track citizens working abroad, and employment agencies must report individuals who do not return from abroad as scheduled.

<u>Exile</u>: The law does not allow forced exile, but sources asserted that security forces continued to threaten some opposition members with bodily harm or prosecution if they did not leave the country, and many were in self-imposed exile.

Many university students who had been expelled or believed themselves to be under the threat of expulsion for their political activities opted for self-imposed exile and continued their studies abroad.

Protection of Refugees

<u>Access to Asylum</u>: The law provides for granting asylum or refugee status, complementary and temporary protection to foreign citizens and stateless persons. The government has established a procedure for determining refugee status and a system for providing protection to refugees. Additionally, the law provides for protection against refoulement, which is granted to foreigners who are denied refugee status or temporary protection, but cannot be returned to their countries of origin.

All foreigners except Russians have the right to apply for asylum. Under the terms of the Union Treaty with Russia, Russians can legally settle and obtain residence permits in the country based on their Russian citizenship and therefore do not need asylum. Overall, as of October 1, immigration authorities accepted 596 applications for asylum compared with more than 1,000 in 2015, including from 443 Ukrainians, 13 Syrians, 22 Afghans, and 20 Tajiks.

In addition to refugee status, the country's asylum law provides for complementary protection and protection against refoulement (in the form of temporary residence for a one-year term). In the period January-September, 428 foreigners were granted complementary protection (395 Ukrainians, seven Syrians, one Libyan, 18 Yemenis, six Iraqi, and one Kyrgyz).

Freedom of Movement: Asylum seekers have freedom of movement within the country but must reside in the region where they filed their applications for refugee status and in a place known to authorities while their applications are being considered, including during appeals. Authorities reportedly often encouraged asylum seekers to settle in rural areas; however, the majority settled in cities and towns. Change of residence was possible with a notification to authorities. Authorities issue registered asylum seekers certificates that serve as documents to confirm their status of asylum-seekers and identity and protect them from expulsion. In accordance with the law, they also must register with local authorities at their place of residence.

Temporary Protection: Although the government may provide temporary protection (for up to one year) to individuals who may not qualify as refugees, it did not do so during the year.

Stateless Persons

As of January 1, the Ministry of the Interior and UNHCR listed 5,635 stateless persons in the country; all had permanent residence according to authorities.

Permanently resident stateless persons held residence permits and were treated comparably to citizens in terms of access to employment, with the exception of a limited number of positions in the public sector and law enforcement that were available only to citizens. There were reports that stateless persons occasionally faced discrimination in employment, since authorities often encouraged them to settle in rural areas where the range of employment opportunities was limited.

According to UNHCR, stateless persons could freely change their region of residence.

There is a path towards nationality or citizenship for this stateless population. The main requirement is at least seven years' permanent residence. Authorities have a procedure for expedited naturalization procedures but mostly for individuals born or permanently residing in the country prior to the collapse of the Soviet Union, ethnic Belarusians, their spouses, and descendants. If a child is born into a family of stateless persons permanently residing in the country, the child is entitled to Belarusian citizenship. The decrease of the number of stateless individuals in the country was attributed to their naturalization.

Section 3. Freedom to Participate in the Political Process

The law provides citizens the ability to choose their government in free and fair periodic elections based on universal and equal suffrage, but the government consistently denied citizens this ability by not conducting elections according to international standards.

Since his election in 1994 to a four-year term as the country's first president, Lukashenka steadily consolidated power in the executive branch to dominate all branches of government, effectively ending any separation of powers among the branches. Flawed referenda in 1996 and 2004 amended the constitution to broaden his powers, extend his term in office, and remove presidential term limits. Subsequent elections, including the presidential elections held in 2015 and parliamentary elections held in September, continued to deny citizens the right to express their will in an honest and transparent process including fair access to media and to resources.

Elections and Political Participation

Recent Elections: The September 11, 2016 parliamentary elections failed to meet international standards. However, for the first time in 12 years, alternative voices were seated in parliament. The elections were marred by a number of long-standing systemic shortcomings, according to the OSCE/ODIHR, the OSCE Parliamentary Assembly, and the Parliamentary Assembly of the Council of Europe international election observation mission intermediate report. While the observer missions and the international community welcomed visible efforts by authorities to make some procedural improvements, a number of key long-standing recommendations by the OSCE/ODIHR and Council of Europe Venice

Commission remained unaddressed, underscoring the need for comprehensive electoral reform as part of the broader democratization process.

The OSCE report found that the legal framework restricts political rights and fundamental freedoms and was interpreted in an overly restrictive manner. While there was an overall increase in the number of candidates, including from the opposition, media coverage did not enable voters to make an informed choice and the campaign lacked visibility. As in past years, only a negligible number of election commission members were appointed from opposition nominees, which undermined confidence in their independence. The early voting, counting, and tabulation procedures continued to be marred by a significant number of procedural irregularities and a lack of transparency.

Out of the 630 nominated candidates, 484 eventually stood for election, including a significant number from the opposition. No candidate was elected unopposed Despite an overall increase in the number of candidates, the legal provisions for candidate registration allowed for selective implementation. Ninety-three prospective candidates were not permitted to register, mostly due to inaccuracies in asset and income declarations, an insufficient number of valid signatures in support of their candidacy, or the failure to submit supporting documentation. This approach was overly restrictive, posing disproportionate and unreasonable barriers to candidacy, the OSCE report read.

According to the OSCE report, restrictions on fundamental freedoms of association, expression, and assembly narrowed the public space and negatively affected the environment in which the elections were held. Although a high number of candidates chose not to campaign actively, contributing to broad voter apathy, most were generally able to campaign freely within the restrictive confines of the law. Unequal access to institutions and resources skewed the playing field for candidates, the OSCE assessed. Several candidates stated that the abolishment of government campaign financing in 2013 reduced their outreach capacities, which limited the choice available to voters and their ability to make an informed decision.

The majority of observers at local polling places appeared to be from government-sponsored NGOs. Many of them reportedly received instructions in advance to report to foreign observers that the proceedings were "in order" or to harass independent observers. These government-sponsored groups did not release any reports on their observation efforts or recommendations on how to improve the process.

The OSCE observation mission reported that during the five-day early voting period, "in 8 percent of the cases the ballot box was not sealed securely and in 45 percent it was not secured in a safe or metal box." Contrary to the law, 16 percent of the observed precinct electoral commissions recorded the aggregated rather than the daily turnout figure in the daily protocols, in 17 percent the daily protocols were not posted publicly, and in some 7 percent of precinct electoral commissions observers were not allowed to make photos of them. At the close of early voting, authorities announced a turnout of 31 percent. The report read that turnout was significantly higher in precinct commissions assigned to voters in state enterprises and public institutions, including student dormitories, where there were credible allegations and observation of voters being coerced to vote. They also noted complaints made by independent domestic observers in a number of polling stations alleging discrepancies between reported turnout and the number of signatures in the voter lists, and inconsistent completion of daily protocols.

According to the OSCE observation mission report, observers assessed the counting process negatively in 24 percent of polling stations observed despite authorities' resolution to enhance observer access to the count. In 27 percent of precinct election commissions, observers were not allowed close to the counting table and to observe without restrictions, and in 8 percent they were not allowed to make photographs of protocols. In many instances international observers reported that the count was hasty and lacked transparency, and in one-quarter of cases observers could not follow the procedures and see voters' marks on the ballots. In approximately 20 percent of polling stations observed, the final result protocols were presigned, the validity of ballots was not determined in a consistent and reasonable manner, and spoiled ballots were not packed up and sealed. The tabulation process was observed in all 110 district electoral commissions and assessed negatively in about one-quarter of observations. In 12 percent of precincts there was a delay in transporting precinct protocols to district commissions. In 16 percent of precincts the data from precinct protocols were not entered in electronic summarized tables, and in 60 percent the data were not entered in ink. In one-half of the district electoral commissions, observers were not close enough to see data being entered and in one-third of cases were not able to observe the entire process. The government did not permit independent organizations to conduct exit polls.

Local human rights groups Vyasna and the Belarusian Helsinki Committee stated at a postelection press conference that based on their observation, the election fell short of international standards and did not fully abide by the country's legislation.

They especially noted their concern with early voting procedures, the lack of transparency in the vote-count process, and the domination of election commissions by progovernment organizations.

Amendments in 2013 to the electoral code introduced a simple majority system in the first round of elections for the National Assembly and ended government funding of campaigns while increasing the allowable amount of private funding. Some members of the democratic opposition alleged that the amendments disproportionately targeted the opposition, which had little access to private funds given President Lukashenka's public statements that businesses should not finance the opposition or they would face punishment. Additionally, the amendments prohibit citizens from campaigning to disrupt elections and referenda or to have them cancelled, postponed, or boycotted. Other changes included regulations on who can appeal for a vote recount and what type of questions can be put to public referendum.

<u>Political Parties and Political Participation</u>: Authorities routinely harassed and impeded the activities of opposition political parties and activists. Some opposition parties lacked legal status because authorities refused to register them, and the government routinely interfered with the right to organize, run for election, seek votes, and publicize views. The government allowed approximately half a dozen largely inactive, but officially registered pro-Lukashenka political parties to operate freely.

On May 6, a Minsk district court fined United Civic Party Chair Anatol Lyabedzka 1,050 rubles ($525) and party members Volha Mayorava and Dzianis Krasochka 630 rubles ($315) each for violating the Law on Mass Events. Police charged the three with holding a picket while illegally distributing printed materials that allegedly contained information against the government, at the entrance of the Minsk Automobile Factory on April 14. Lyabedzka noted during the trial that under the Law on Political Parties registered parties are "from the moment of registration entitled to freely spread the information on their activities, advocate their ideas, aims and decisions."

The law allows authorities to suspend parties for six months after one warning and close them after two. During the year political parties did not receive any formal warnings, but members of parties that authorities refused to register, such as the Belarus Christian Democracy Party, continued to be subjected to harassment and arbitrary checks. The law also prohibits political parties from receiving support from abroad and requires all political groups and coalitions to register with the Ministry of Justice.

Authorities continued to limit activities of the unrecognized Union of Poles of Belarus and harass its members.

<u>Participation of Women and Minorities</u>: No laws prevent women or minorities from voting or participating in political life on the same basis as men or nonminority citizens. In 2015 Tatsiana Karatkevich was the first woman to run for president, and on election day President Lukashenka told the press, "our president has numerous functions, from security to the economy. A person in a skirt is unlikely to be able to cope with them now." He added that even if this were not the case, society was not ready for a female president.

Section 4. Corruption and Lack of Transparency in Government

The law provides criminal penalties for official corruption, and the government regularly jailed officials alleged to be corrupt; however, reports indicated officials continued to engage in corrupt practices. The World Bank's Worldwide Governance Indicators reflected that corruption was a serious problem in the country.

On September 1, the Group of States against Corruption (GRECO) released a summary of the interim compliance report, which said that the government partially implemented only one of the 20 recommendations made by the Council of Europe's anticorruption monitoring body in June 2015. The one recommendation was reportedly related to the introduction of administrative liability of legal persons for money-laundering offenses. GRECO noted the "lack of an evidence-based comprehensive strategy and plan of action for the fight against corruption, and of a mechanism that does not only involve the law enforcement agencies to monitor its implementation independently, comprehensively and objectively." GRECO expressed disappointment regarding the significant volume of information submitted by the government, which was not relevant for the purpose of assessing the country's compliance with the anti-corruption recommendations. The summary also noted that no concrete projects, which could significantly contribute to the elimination of corruption in the country, seemed to be under way and that "it looks as if the process of implementation of improvements has been halted." The full report was not available because the government did not consent to its publication.

In July 2015 the president signed into law anticorruption legislation, which came into force on January 24 and reportedly strengthened existing anticorruption regulations. Under the amended law, individuals dismissed for lower-level corruption face a five-year ban on public-service employment, while those found to have committed more serious abuses are banned indefinitely from government employment. The law also allows seizure of property worth more than 25 percent of a public servant's yearly income for those found guilty of corrupt practices. The amendments also introduced provisions for public monitoring of the government's anticorruption efforts.

Corruption: According to official sources, most corruption cases involved soliciting and accepting bribes, fraud, and abuse of power, although anecdotal evidence indicated such corruption usually did not occur as part of day-to-day interaction between citizens and minor state officials.

The absence of an independent judicial system and law enforcement, the lack of separation of powers, and a harried independent press largely barred from interaction with a nontransparent state bureaucracy made it virtually impossible to gauge the scale of corruption or combat it effectively.

The Prosecutor General's Office is responsible for organizing and coordinating activities to combat corruption, including monitoring law enforcement operations, analyzing the efficacy of implemented measures, supervising engaged parties, and drafting further legislation.

The Prosecutor General's Office reported that from January to May courts heard 451 corruption cases compared with 533 cases in the same period in 2015. Of these, 50 related to offering or accepting bribes. The most corrupt sectors were state administration and procurement, the industrial sector, the construction industry, health care, and education.

The Prosecutor General's Office reported that authorities investigated 1,603 corruption-related crimes in 2015. Of those, 673 were cases related to bribery, 572 cases of embezzlement, and 346 cases related to abuse of powers.

There were numerous corruption prosecutions during the year, but prosecutions remained selective, nontransparent, and in some cases appeared politically motivated, according to independent observers and human rights advocates.

On March 1, authorities sentenced Vyachaslau Pakholchyk, a former head of the local executive authorities in the town of Uzda, to seven years in prison and forfeiture of his property on a charge of accepting a bribe of approximately 31,500 rubles ($15,000). Pakholchyk was also banned from serving in administrative positions for a period of five years.

Financial Disclosure: Anticorruption laws require income and asset disclosure by appointed and elected officials, their spouses, and members of households who have reached legal age and continue to live with them in the same household. According to the law, specialized anticorruption departments within the Prosecutor General's Office, the KGB, and the Internal Affairs Ministry monitor and verify anticorruption practices, and the prosecutor general and all other prosecutors are mandated to oversee the enforcement of anticorruption law. These declarations were not made available to the public. An exception applies to candidates running in presidential, parliamentary, and municipal elections. There are administrative sanctions and disciplinary penalties for noncompliance.

Public Access to Information: The law, government policies, and a presidential decree severely restricted public access to government information. Citizens had some access to certain categories of information on government databases and websites, but much of the information was neither current nor complete.

Section 5. Governmental Attitude Regarding International and Nongovernmental Investigation of Alleged Violations of Human Rights

There were a number of active domestic human rights NGOs, although authorities were often hostile to their efforts, selectively cooperated with them, and were not responsive to their views.

Two prominent human rights NGOs--the Belarusian Helsinki Committee and the Center for Legal Transformations--were registered. The government refused to register others, placing them at risk under the criminal code, which criminalizes organizing, or participating in any activity by, an unregistered organization. The law also prohibits persons from acting on behalf of unregistered NGOs. Nonetheless, a variety of unregistered NGOs, including Vyasna, the Solidarity Committee for the Protection of the Repressed, and Legal Assistance to the Population, continued to operate.

Authorities harassed both registered and unregistered human rights organizations, subjected them to frequent inspections and threats of deregistration, reportedly monitored their correspondence and telephone conversations, and harassed family members of group leaders and activists. The government ignored reports issued by human rights NGOs and rarely met with them. State-run media did not report on human rights NGOs and their actions.

In February 2015 authorities expelled Alena Tankachova, a Russian citizen, from the country and stated she would not be permitted to return for three years. Tankachova, the chair of the Legal Transformation Center (also called Lawtrend), had been a permanent resident for 30 years. Authorities accused her of traffic violations and stated she posed a threat to national security. Local human rights organizations asserted the case was politically motivated and that she was expelled for her human rights work. On October 24, the Interior Ministry denied Tankachova's October 5 appeal to remove the entry ban against her.

During the year the Belarusian Helsinki Committee's bank accounts remained blocked due to long-standing tax arrears related to foreign funding in the early 2000s, but the government allowed the committee to operate without other interference.

Authorities were reluctant to engage on human rights problems with international human rights NGOs or other human rights officials, and international NGO representatives often had difficulty gaining admission to the country.

Authorities routinely ignored local and international groups' recommendations on improving human rights in the country and requests to stop harassing the human rights community.

Authorities can close an NGO after issuing only one warning that it violated the law. The most common pretexts prompting a warning or closure were failure to obtain a legal address and technical discrepancies in application documents. The law allows authorities to close an NGO for accepting what it considered illegal forms of foreign assistance and permits the Ministry of Justice to participate in any NGO activity and to review all NGO documents. NGOs also must submit detailed reports annually to the ministry about their activities, office locations, officers, and total number of members.

<u>The United Nations or Other International Bodies</u>: In July the UN Human Rights Council extended the mandate of Miklos Haraszti as the special rapporteur on the human rights situation in Belarus. During the year Haraszti released three reports on the situation of human rights in the country. Senior foreign ministry officials continued to assert Haraszti's mandate was "politically motivated" and that his appointment was made "without consultations and approval from Belarusian

authorities." The government continued to refuse any cooperation with his mission, and he was not permitted to enter the country.

Government Human Rights Bodies: On October 24, Deputy Foreign Minister Alena Kupchyna announced that the government adopted a national human rights action plan and described it as, "a political document and a kind of a road map to outline main activities for us to implement our international obligations" on human rights. The government published, "the interagency plan to implement the 2016-2019 Universal Periodic Review recommendations" on October 25. While independent human rights groups, including the human rights center Vyasna and the Belarusian Helsinki Committee (BHC), welcomed the plan's adoption, they also noted with concern that the documents lacks specific target goals or results assessment mechanisms. They noted that the government failed to include any of the concrete suggestions civil society groups offered during the drafting of the plan, which they believe would have made the plan more substantial.

A standing commission on human rights in the lower chamber of parliament was ineffective.

Section 6. Discrimination, Societal Abuses, and Trafficking in Persons

Women

Rape and Domestic Violence: The law criminalizes rape in general but does not include separate provisions on marital rape. Rape was a problem, but most victims did not report it due to shame or fear that police would blame the victim. According to the Ministry of Internal Affairs, there were 145 registered cases of rape or attempted rape in 2015.

Domestic violence was a significant problem, and the government took measures to prevent it during the year, although it yet again postponed adoption of a comprehensive law on domestic violence.

The government directed efforts to combat gender-based violence mainly by preventing such crimes and not by protecting or assisting victims, although crisis rooms provided limited psychological and medical assistance to victims.

As of January the state operated 109 shelter-type crisis rooms for victims, including domestic violence victims; NGOs operated at least three more shelters for victims of domestic violence. Authorities reported that in 2015 crisis rooms assisted 237 individuals, including 178 domestic violence victims; however, observers noted a lack of adequate staff training, short-term sheltering, limited working hours, and unsafe locations.

A 2014 law on preventing crimes establishes a separate definition of domestic violence and provides for implementation of protective orders. Such orders, ranging from three to 30 days' duration, are issued to abusers who have been charged with two counts of violence within one year. The law requires authorities to provide victims and abusers with temporary accommodation until the protection orders expire. In addition to the newly adopted law, the code on administrative offenses, amended in 2013, prescribes a large fine or detention for up to 15 days for battery, intended infliction of pain, and psychological or physical suffering committed against a close family member. The criminal code does not contain a separate article dealing specifically with domestic violence.

Police reported that, from January to October 2015, they identified 1,984 victims of domestic violence; of those 1,509 were female, 475 were male, and 120 were older than age 70. Ninety-six victims of domestic violence died, and 169 suffered severe bodily injuries in 2015. In the majority of these cases, women said they had been previously threatened with violence. Additionally, police investigated more than 42,000 allegations of domestic violence from January to October 2015. The police official reported that women were the aggressors in at least 10 percent of all domestic violence cases and were responsible for approximately 35 percent of all murders and incidents of severe bodily harm connected to domestic violence.

According to a 2014 UN Population Fund study, three out of four women and men between the ages of 18 and 60 claimed they had been subject to some form of domestic violence. Of this number, 76 percent of women and 76 percent of men had been subject to psychological violence, and 37 percent of women and 28 percent of men had been subject to economic pressures. More than 31 percent of women and 24 percent of men suffered from physical violence, and 18 percent of women and 12 percent of men reported their partners sexually abused them. Women remained reluctant to report domestic violence due to fear of escalating the violence, reprisal, social stigma, and a lack of confidence they would receive appropriate and timely assistance. Moreover, they feared that if the aggressor were fined, the financial burden would fall on the family. Male victims of domestic violence did not report their cases due to their own feelings of guilt, feeling pity for their abuser, and fear of family disruptions. According to the study, 12 percent of male and 29 percent of female victims of domestic violence sought professional assistance.

<u>Sexual Harassment</u>: Sexual harassment reportedly was widespread, but no specific laws, other than those against physical assault, address the problem.

<u>Reproductive Rights</u>: Couples and individuals have the right to decide the number, spacing, and timing of children; manage their reproductive health; and have access to the information and means to do so, free from discrimination, coercion, or violence. Access to information on contraception and skilled attendance at delivery and in postpartum care were widely available. The UN Population Division estimated 55 percent of girls and women ages 15-49 used a modern method of contraception in 2015.

<u>Discrimination</u>: The law provides for equal treatment of women with regard to property ownership and inheritance, family law, equal pay for equal work (although in practice women were often paid less), and in the judicial system, and the law was generally respected.

Women's groups voiced concerns about the increasing percentage of women in poverty, particularly among women with more than two children, female-headed households, women taking care of family members with disabilities or older family members, rural women, and older women.

Children

<u>Birth Registration</u>: Citizenship is derived either by birth within the country's territory or from one's parents. A child of a citizen is a citizen regardless of place of birth, even if one of the parents is not a citizen. In general, births were registered immediately.

<u>Child Abuse</u>: The government continued to implement a 2012-16 comprehensive national plan to improve childcare and the protection of children's rights, including for victims of child abuse, domestic violence, and commercial sexual exploitation, and acknowledged a lack of funding and inefficiency in executing certain protective measures. With assistance from NGOs that promote children's rights, authorities extensively employed procedures for on-the-record, one-time interviewing of child abuse victims in the framework of investigations or criminal cases at specialized facilities under the direct supervision of psychologists. Courts used recorded testimony to avoid repeatedly summoning child abuse victims for hearings. Cases that affected the rights and legitimate interests of minors were generally heard by more experienced judges with expertise in developmental psychology, psychiatry, and education. The government failed to resume

operations of a national hotline for assisting children despite various NGOs' requests to support the hotline.

As of January the Ministry of Education ran 138 social-educational centers nationwide for minor victims of any type of violence or minors finding themselves in vulnerable and dangerous conditions. Centers could provide short-term shelter, food, clothing, personal hygiene products, and medical and psychological aid to victims. No data on the number of assisted child abuse victims at these centers was available. General healthcare institutions provided a wide range of medical aid to child abuse victims free of charge.

Authorities intervened to prevent child abuse stemming from domestic violence and identified families in vulnerable conditions, providing foster care to children who could not be kept with their immediate families while preventive work was underway. Although the government increased prosecution of child abusers, its efforts to address the causes of child abuse were inadequate.

Rape or sexual assault of a person known to be a minor is punishable by up to 15 years in jail. Sexual acts between a person older than 18 and a person known to be younger than 16 carry penalties of up to five years in jail.

From January to October 2015, authorities registered 193 pedophilia crimes, including 18 cases of rape, 74 cases of coercive actions of a sexual nature, 87 cases of sexual intercourse with a minor, and 14 cases of sexual abuse. Police identified 135 victims of pedophilia, including 58 children under 14, mostly female, in 2015.

Early and Forced Marriage: The legal minimum age of marriage for both boys and girls is 18 years old, although girls as young as 14 can be married legally with parental consent. There were reports of early marriage in which girls as young as 14 and boys as young as 16 married with parental consent.

Sexual Exploitation of Children: The minimum age for consensual sex is 16. Prostitution of children was a problem. From January to October 2015, the Internal Affairs Ministry investigated 506 crimes involving the commercial sexual exploitation of children, including 25 cases of the production and distribution of child pornography and six cases in which minors became victims of trafficking for sexual exploitation. The law provides penalties of up to 13 years in prison for production or distribution of pornographic materials depicting a minor. The law generally was enforced.

<u>Institutionalized Children</u>: There was no system for monitoring child abuse in orphanages or other specialized institutions. Authorities did not publicly report on any child abuse incidents in institutions. There were allegations of abuse in foster families. The government opened or continued investigations into some of these cases.

<u>International Child Abductions</u>: The country is a party to the 1980 Hague Convention on the Civil Aspects of International Child Abduction. See the Department of State's *Annual Report on International parental Child Abduction* at travel.state.gov/content/childabduction/en/legal/compliance.html.

Anti-Semitism

Jewish groups estimated that between 30,000 and 40,000 persons identified themselves as Jews. Most were not active religiously.

Anti-Semitic incidents continued but were on the decline; authorities sporadically investigated reports of such acts. Jewish community and civil society activists expressed concern over the concept of a "greater Slavic union" that was popular among nationalist organizations, including the neo-Nazi group Russian National Unity, which remained active despite its official dissolution in 2000. Neo-Nazis were widely believed to be behind anti-Semitic incidents across the country. Anti-Semitic and Russian ultranationalist newspapers, literature, DVDs, and videotapes imported from Russia were widely available. The government did not promote antibias and tolerance education.

On May 25, authorities in Valozhyn opened a criminal case to investigate vandalism of a memorial in honor of 800 local Jews killed in 1942 near the town of Ivianets. Part of the plaque was broken and a swastika was painted on the fence of the memorial. There were no reported developments in the case.

On July 9, local Jewish community members reported that they saw yellow paint on sculptures at the Holocaust memorial called "Yama" (the Pit) dedicated to the Minsk ghetto victims. Authorities opened an investigation after appeals from the National Union of Jewish Communities and Organizations, but no developments were reported.

On September 21, the government signed a cultural heritage agreement that encourages efforts to "preserve and protect certain cultural properties of all ethnic groups, including the victims of the Nazi genocide."

In November the country hosted the Conference of European Rabbis. The conference participants discussed cooperation on erecting monuments and other issues with senior officials, including the speaker of the upper chamber of the parliament and the plenipotentiary representative for religious and nationalities affairs.

Local journalists and Jewish activists reported on November 19 that unidentified vandals sprayed black paint on a monument commemorating thousands of Jews who were killed by Nazis in the local ghetto during the Holocaust in Mahilyou. Police reportedly opened a criminal case and on November 22 detained four individuals, who reportedly expressed ultra-right Nazi ideas and belonged to a local skinhead group. Leaders of the local Jewish community cleaned the monument on November 20. The monument had also been defaced in 2012. The police did not convict anyone in 2012, claiming that someone spilled paint by accident.

On November 30, local police in the city of Pinsk opened an investigation into vandalism of a memorial honoring Jewish and Roma victims of the Holocaust as well as commemorating killings of prisoners, partisans and underground fighters by the Nazis in 1941-44. Unidentified vandals painted a swastika on the plaque of the memorial, which was installed on the site of the former Jewish ghetto in central Pinsk.

Trafficking in Persons

See the Department of State's *Trafficking in Persons Report* at www.state.gov/j/tip/rls/tiprpt/.

Persons with Disabilities

The law does not specifically prohibit discrimination against persons with physical, sensory, intellectual, or mental disabilities in employment, education, air travel and other transportation, access to health care, and other government services; discrimination was common.

The Ministry of Labor and Social Security is the main government agency responsible for protecting the rights of persons with disabilities. The law mandates that transport, residences, and businesses be accessible to persons with disabilities, but few public areas were wheelchair accessible or accessible for hearing and vision-impaired persons. The National Association of Disabled Wheelchair Users estimated that more than 90 percent of persons with physical disabilities were unable to leave their places of residence without assistance and stated their residences were not built to accommodate persons with physical disabilities. While authorities claimed that 30 percent of the country's total infrastructure was accessible, disability rights organizations considered this figure inflated.

The country's lack of independent living opportunities left many persons with disabilities no choice but to live in state-run institutions. Approximately 80 such institutions across the country housed more than 10,000 persons. Disability rights organizations reported that the quality of care in these facilities was low, and instances of fundamental human rights violations, harassment, mistreatment, and other abuse were reported. Authorities frequently placed persons with physical and mental disabilities in the same facilities and did not provide either group with specialized care.

Public transportation was free to persons with disabilities, but the majority of subway stations in Minsk and the bus system were not wheelchair accessible. According to government statistics, 5 percent of the country's public transportation network was accessible.

Disability rights organizations reported difficulty organizing advocacy activities due to impediments to freedom of assembly, censorship, and the government's unwillingness to register assistance projects (see section 2.b.).

Advocates also noted that persons with disabilities, especially those with vision and hearing disabilities, lacked the ability to address violations of their rights easily and completely since courts often failed to provide access and sign language interpretation. Separately, women with disabilities often faced discrimination with respect to their reproductive rights, and there were reports of authorities attempting to take children away from families in which parents had disabilities, claiming that the parents would not be able to provide appropriate care of their children. In addition, women with disabilities, as well as women, whose children were diagnosed with potential disabilities in utero reported that some doctors insisted they terminate their pregnancies.

National/Racial/Ethnic Minorities

Governmental and societal discrimination against Roma persisted. There were also expressions of societal hostility toward proponents of the local national culture, which the government often identified with actors of the democratic opposition, repeatedly labeled by President Lukashenka as "the fifth column."

Authorities continued to harass the independent and unregistered Union of Poles of Belarus.

Official and societal discrimination continued against the country's 7,000 (according to the 2009 census) to 60,000 Roma (according to Romani community estimates). The Romani community continued to experience marginalization, various types of discrimination, high unemployment, low levels of education, and lack of access to social services. Generally, Roma hold Belarusian citizenship, but many lacked official government identity documents and refused to obtain them.

An independent survey, conducted by Romani communities and experts of the state-run Center for National Cultures in 2014, estimated that no more than 2 percent of the Roma had university education and that only 17 percent enrolled in vocational training after junior high school. Twelve percent of Roma older than age 10 remained illiterate. Only 9 percent of Roma were officially employed. There continued to be isolated reports that non-Romani children and teachers harassed Romani children, which forced Romani families to withdraw their children from schools. The majority of Romani youth did not finish secondary school and failed to enroll in university programs, although the situation continued to improve as more Romani children from mixed families enrolled and obtained bachelor degrees, including in areas outside of Minsk. There were no special school programs for Roma, although there were such programs for Jews, ethnic Lithuanians, and Poles.

In April 2015 the website of the regional newspaper *Avangard* in Buda-Kashaliova published an article that associated Roma with criminal activities and contained a police warning to residents to report "suspicious activity." Local activists Maryia Klimovich and Ales Yauseyenka raised concerns about the article through media outlets. In February Klimovich and Yauseyenka appealed to the Ministry of the Interior to stop publication of police accusations that Romani representatives were behind criminal activity. In its March response to the activists, the ministry's press office dismissed the claims and stated, "the public mention of ethnicity of any criminals did not incite any hatred." The ministry added, "the negative reaction to such publications could be taken as lobbying interests of the Roma to avoid liability for their criminal activity."

According to leaders of the Romani communities, security and law enforcement agencies arbitrarily detained, investigated, and harassed Roma, including by forced fingerprinting, maltreatment in detention, and ethnic insults. In March 2015 the Belarusian Helsinki Committee sent an inquiry to the Interior Ministry and the General Prosecutor's Office, raising their concerns about human rights violations against the Roma and seeking a stop to police discrimination. The agencies reportedly studied cases of maltreatment, and Romani leaders stated the situation continued to improve during the year as authorities took measures to prevent discrimination and worked closely with Romani "mediators" to integrate marginalized community members.

While the Russian and Belarusian languages have equal legal status, Russian was the primary language of government. According to independent polling, the overwhelming majority of the population spoke Russian as their mother tongue. Because the government viewed many proponents of the Belarusian language as political opponents, authorities continued to harass and intimidate academic and cultural groups that sought to promote Belarusian and routinely rejected proposals to widen use of the language, although the situation improved before year's end.

Acts of Violence, Discrimination, and Other Abuses Based on Sexual Orientation and Gender Identity

Consensual same-sex sexual conduct between adults is not illegal, but discrimination against LGBTI persons was widespread, and harassment occurred.

Due to egregious official harassment of the LGBTI community, groups opted for holding private activities and events. LGBTI groups did not seek permission from authorities to hold any public events. Mikhail Pishcheuski, a gay man who was harassed and severely beaten as he left a club in Minsk in 2014, died from his injuries in October 2015. The main perpetrator of the assault, Dzmitry Lukashevich, was convicted of hooliganism and inflicting severe bodily harm in 2014 and was sentenced to two years and eight months in prison. Although Lukashevich was released as part of the government's amnesty program in September 2015, ultimately serving only 11 months in prison, prosecutors reopened a criminal case against him after Pishcheuski's death on the charges of negligent homicide and hooliganism. A Minsk district court sentenced him to three years in prison on July 28. Pishcheuski's mother, sister, and brother, also sued Lukashevich for damages totaling 210,000 rubles ($100,000), but the judge reduced the damages to 21,000 rubles ($10,000) total, noting that Lukashevich would not be capable of paying such a large sum.

On June 10, a regional court in Homyel convicted 11 young men of beating and abusing a gay man in May 2015. Ten of them were charged with hooliganism and received suspended sentences, and one of the abusers, who had a previous criminal record, was jailed for four years and two months. The 11 men,, calling themselves "anti-pedophile" activists, lured the 27-year-old victim into an apartment, beat him, undressed him, painted a swastika and explicit language on his body, and forced him to walk outside naked.

In a conviction on February 10, a Minsk district court sentenced a man to two years of restricted freedom (similar to partial house arrest) and ordered him to compensate his victim 500 rubles ($230) in damages for assaulting an LGBTI person because of his sexual orientation. The court based its conviction on an article of criminal code that covers crimes based on hatred "toward a certain social group." This was the first time this provision of the criminal code had been used to prosecute crimes against LGBTI victims. According to the LGBTI human rights NGO Identity, the defendant contacted the victim on an LGBTI-focused social network website and later met the victim in November 2015. The defendant questioned the victim to confirm the latter was gay and then hit him several times, stole his cell phone and some cash, and threatened to post a video of the beating unless the victim changed his sexual orientation. The defendant admitted to authorities that he had been "hunting" for LGBTI individuals online, with the goal of forcing them to change their sexual identities. Independent human rights groups welcomed the verdict.

Societal discrimination against LGBTI activists persisted with the tacit support of the regime. The police continued to mistreat LGBTI persons and refused to investigate crimes against LGBTI persons. A number of individuals filed complaints, but police refused to open investigations during the year.

The government does not provide transgender persons with new national identification numbers, which include a digit that signifies gender. Transgender persons reportedly have been refused jobs when potential employers note the "discrepancy" between the identification number and the stated gender of the applicant. Banks also refused to open accounts for transgender persons on the same grounds.

HIV and AIDS Social Stigma

Societal discrimination against persons with HIV/AIDS remained a problem, and the illness carried a heavy social stigma. The Joint UN Program on HIV/AIDS reported there were numerous reports of HIV-infected individuals who faced discrimination, especially at workplaces and during job interviews.

There were also frequent reports of family discrimination against HIV/AIDS-positive relatives, including preventing HIV/AIDS-positive parents from seeing their children or requiring HIV/AIDS-positive family members to use separate dishware. Authorities also reported that a few HIV-positive orphans remained institutionalized due to families' reluctance to adopt or foster children with HIV/AIDS.

The government continued to broadcast and post public service advertisements raising awareness about HIV/AIDS and calling for greater tolerance toward persons infected with the virus.

Section 7. Worker Rights

a. Freedom of Association and the Right to Collective Bargaining

Although the law provides for the rights of workers, except state security and military personnel, to form and join independent unions and to strike, it places a number of serious restrictions on the exercise of these rights. The law provides for the right to organize and bargain collectively but does not protect against antiunion discrimination. Workers who say they are fired for union activity have no explicit right to reinstatement or to challenge their dismissal in court, according to independent union activists.

The government did not enforce civil penalties in the form of fines for violations of the freedom of assembly or collective bargaining, which according to local worker rights advocates, were not sufficient to deter violations.

The government severely restricted independent unions. The government-controlled Federation of Trade Unions of Belarus is the largest union, claiming more than four million members, although that number was inflated, since the country's total workforce was approximately four million. It largely resembled its Soviet predecessors and served as a control mechanism and distributor of benefits. The Belarusian Congress of Democratic Trade Unions (BCDTU), with four constituent unions and approximately 10,000 members of independent trade unions, was the largest independent union umbrella organization, but tight government control over registration requirements and public demonstrations made it difficult for the Congress to organize, expand, and strike.

Government did not respect freedom of association and collective bargaining. Prohibitive registration requirements that any new independent union have a large membership and cooperation from the employer continued to present significant obstacles to union formation. Trade unions may be deleted from the register by a decision of the registrar, without any court procedure. The registrar can remove a trade union from the register if, following the issuance of a written warning to the trade union stating that the organization violates legislation or its own statues, the violations are not eliminated within a month. Authorities continued to resist attempts by workers to leave the official union and join the independent one.

The legal requirements to conduct a strike are high. For example, strikes can only be held at least three months after dispute resolution between the union and employer has failed. The duration of the strike must be specified in advance. Additionally, a minimum number of workers must continue to work during the strike. Nevertheless, these requirements were largely irrelevant, since the unions that represented almost all workers were under government control. Government authorities and managers of state-owned enterprises routinely interfered with union activities and hindered workers' efforts to bargain collectively, in some instances arbitrarily suspending collective bargaining agreements. Management and local authorities blocked worker attempts to organize strikes on many occasions by declaring them illegal. Union members who participated in unauthorized public demonstrations were subjected to arrest and detention. Due to a persistent atmosphere of repression and the fear of imprisonment, few public demonstrations took place during the year.

The Law on Mass Events also seriously limited demonstrations, rallies, and other public action, constraining the right of unions to organize and strike. No foreign assistance may be offered to trade unions for holding seminars, meetings, strikes, pickets etc., or for "propaganda activities" aimed at their own members, without the authorities' permission.

On May 20, a court in Baranavichy sentenced Aliaksandr Shved, a member of the independent Belarusian Union of Electronic Industry Workers, to a fine of 420 rubles ($210) for violating the Law on Mass Events when he participated in an unsanctioned protest in support of a dismissed associate on March 31. Shved claimed in court that he did not participate in the actual protest and was only distributing trade union leaflets.

Government efforts to suppress independent unions included frequent refusals to extend employment contracts for members of independent unions and refusals to register independent unions. According to BCDTU leader Aliaksandr Yarashuk, no independent unions have been established since a 1999 decree requiring trade unions to register with the government. Authorities routinely fired workers who were deemed "natural leaders" or who involved themselves in NGOs or opposition political activities.

In August a state-owned factory in Slonim allegedly dismissed Mikhail Soshka, a member of the independent labor union, over his activities to advocate for workers' rights. Soshka worked at the factory for 30 years and was fired after his travel to Sweden for training at the invitation of a local labor union. He argued that, under the collective bargaining agreement, workers of his age who have less than three years before their retirement should have their employment contracts extended automatically by law. Higher courts dismissed his numerous appeals during the year.

The government requires state employees, including employees of state-owned enterprises, who constituted approximately 70 percent of the workforce, to sign short-term work contracts. Although such contracts may have terms of up to five years, most expired after one year, which gave the government the ability to fire employees by declining to renew their contracts. Many members of independent unions, political parties, and civil society groups lost their jobs because of this practice. A government edict provides the possibility for employers to sign open-ended work contracts with an employee after five years of good conduct by the employee. The edict limits the right of employers to approve open-ended contracts earlier than five years after the service computation date.

Opposition political party members and democratic activists sometimes had difficulty finding work due to government pressure on employers to force them out because of their political engagement and activity. The Belarusian Popular Front opposition party reported in June that their member Volha Damaskina, head of their branch in Navapolatsk, was dismissed from her job of the head of the local museum of traditional hand weaving after announcing that she would run for parliament in the September elections.

In 2014, Lukashenka passed Decree No. 5 On Strengthening the Requirements for Managers and Employees of Organizations, which the authorities stated was aimed at rooting out "mismanagement," strengthening discipline, and preventing the hiring of dishonest managers in new positions. Among other subjects under the new decree, managers can reduce payment of bonuses to employees (which often comprised a large portion of salaries), while workers can be fired more easily. An

independent trade union lawyer told the press that workers have fewer rights under
the new law.

b. Prohibition of Forced or Compulsory Labor

The law prohibits all forms of forced or compulsory labor, but the government did
not effectively enforce its provisions.

Parents who have had their parental rights stripped and are unemployed, or are
working but fail to compensate state childcare facilities for the maintenance of
their children, are subject to forced employment by court order. Individuals who
refuse forced employment may be held criminally liable and face community
service or corrective labor for a period of up to two years, imprisonment for up to
three years, or other freedom restrictions, all involving compulsory labor while
having 70 percent of their wages retained to compensate expenses incurred by the
government.

In January 2010 the government enforced procedures for placing individuals
suffering from chronic alcohol, drug or other substance abuse in so-called medical
labor centers when they have been found guilty of committing criminal violations
while under the influence of alcohol, narcotics and psychotropic, toxic or other
intoxicating substances. Such offenders can be held in these centers by court
orders for a period of 12 to 18 months. These individuals are mandated to work at
these facilities; if they refuse, they can be penalized in solitary confinement for up
to 10 days.

An April 2015 presidential decree, On preventing Social Parasitism, which aims to
force individuals to find employment, established a supplemental tax on persons
who worked less than six months during the year of up to 360 rubles ($200)
annually, depending on how much they paid in taxes when working. The decree
applies to all permanent residents, with senior pensioners, legal minors, persons
with disabilities, and certain other groups exempted. In November 2015 the lower
chamber of the parliament introduced penalties for failing to pay the so-called
"social parasitism" tax, ranging from a fine to short-term arrest, which could
include court-ordered public community service.

Minsk authorities issued provisions in May 2015 requiring officially registered
unemployed individuals to perform paid community service two days a month
from May to September and one day a month from January to April and October to
December. In addition, they were banned from receiving an unemployment benefit

of up to 42 rubles ($21) a month, depending on their length of unemployment. Individuals with disabilities, single parents and parents of three and more children, as well as parents of children with disabilities and under 18 years of age were exempt.

Forced labor regulations were seldom enforced, and resources and inspections dedicated to preventing forced and compulsory labor were minimal and inadequate to deter violations. Penalties for violations included forfeiture of assets and sentences of five to 15 years' imprisonment. The government rarely identified victims of trafficking, and prosecution of those responsible for forced labor remained minimal. Government efforts to prevent and eliminate forced labor in the country did not improve.

Forced labor occurred among men, women, and children. The government prevented state workers in wood processing and related renovation projects from leaving their jobs without employer approval and subjected them to significant fines, such as the repayment of bonuses or benefits, although authorities revoked the decree enforcing these requirements in May.

The government continued the practice of "subbotniks," which require employees of the government, state enterprises, and many private businesses to work on Saturday and donate their earnings to finance government social and other projects. Employers and authorities intimidated and fined some workers who refused to participate.

Authorities reportedly forced military conscripts to perform work unrelated to their military service.

Prison labor practices amounted to forced labor. Former inmates stated that their monthly wages were as low as three to four rubles ($1.5 to $2). Senior officials with the General Prosecutor's Office and the Interior Ministry stated in November 2015 that at least 97 percent of all work-capable inmates worked in jail as required by law, excluding retirees and persons with disabilities, and that labor in jail was important and useful for rehabilitation and reintegration of inmates. Authorities also continued to employ unpaid agricultural labor, ordering university and high school students to help farmers during the harvesting season.

Also see the Department of State's *Trafficking in Persons Report* at www.state.gov/j/tip/rls/tiprpt/.

c. Prohibition of Child Labor and Minimum Age for Employment

The minimum age for employment is 16, but children as young as 14 may conclude a labor contract with the written consent of one parent or a legal guardian. The Prosecutor General's Office is responsible for enforcement of the law. Persons under the age of 18 are allowed to work in nonhazardous jobs but are not allowed to work overtime, on weekends, or on government holidays. Work may not be harmful to children's health or hinder their education.

The government generally enforced these laws, and penalties, ranging from fines and reprimands to 12 years in jail were sufficient to deter most violations. Nevertheless, schoolchildren occasionally continued to be induced to help local collective state-owned farms with the harvest from August to October. On September 29, a 13-year-old hearing-impaired schoolgirl was crushed to death by a truck loaded with potatoes in a field where schoolchildren were collecting the harvest in the Maladzyechna region. Her father filed an appeal to the labor inspection and prosecutors to investigate the case and claim damages. His appeal was denied; he subsequently appealed to the relevant court. According to the head of the farm, local authorities sent as many as 80 schoolchildren to harvest on September 29, and authorities charged the truck driver with reckless driving that resulted in a death. On November 15, the Ministry of Education stated it warned local authorities against using child labor for agricultural works and did not elaborate whether any officials, including teachers and municipal public servants, would be charged in connection with the incident. On December 23, a court sentenced the truck driver to three years of "restricted freedom" for causing death by careless driving and banned him from driving any vehicles for five years.

d. Discrimination with Respect to Employment and Occupation

The law prohibits discrimination based on race, gender, language, or social status. These laws do not apply specifically to employment or occupation. The government did not effectively enforce these laws or secure any effective penalties to deter violations. Discrimination in employment and occupation occurred with respect to ethnicity, gender, disability, language, sexual orientation and/or gender identity and expression, and HIV-positive status (see section 6). In addition, some members of the Romani community complained that employers often discriminated against them and either refused to employ them or did not provide fulltime jobs. The government did not take any action during the year to prevent or eliminate employment discrimination. Employment discrimination happened across most economic sectors and in both private and public workplaces.

The law requiring equal pay for equal work was not regularly enforced, and the minister of labor and social welfare stated on June 21 that on average women were paid 24 percent less than men.

Very few women were in the upper ranks of management or government, and most women were concentrated in the lower-paid public sector. Although the law grants women the right to three years of maternity leave with assurance of job availability upon return, employers often circumvented employment protections by using short-term contracts, then refusing to renew a woman's contract when she became pregnant.

A government prohibition against workdays longer than seven hours for persons with disabilities reportedly made companies reluctant to hire them. Local NGOs reported that up to 85 percent of persons with disabilities were unemployed. Authorities provided minimal welfare benefits for persons with disabilities, and calculations of pensions did not consider disability status. Members of the country's Paralympic teams received half the salaries and prize money of athletes without disabilities.

e. Acceptable Conditions of Work

As of August 1, the national minimum monthly wage was 239.18 rubles ($125). As of September 1, the average monthly wage was 750.3 rubles ($391). As of August 1, the government set the poverty line at 175.5 rubles ($91.40) per month per capita.

The law establishes a standard workweek of 40 hours and provides for at least one 24-hour rest period per week. The law provides for mandatory overtime and holiday pay and restricts overtime to 10 hours a week, with a maximum of 180 hours of overtime each year.

The law establishes minimum conditions for workplace safety and worker health, but employers often ignored these standards. Workers at many heavy machinery plants did not wear minimal safety gear. The state labor inspectorate lacked authority to enforce employer compliance and often ignored violations.

The Ministry of Labor and Social Welfare was responsible for enforcement of these laws. Information regarding resources, inspections, remediation, and penalties was not available. The government reported that approximately 400,000 persons worked in the informal economy. The law did not cover informal workers.

The labor ministry reported 63 persons killed at workplaces between January and June in 2015. The ministry reported the majority of workplace accidents occurred in the heavy machinery production industry and were caused by carelessness, poor conditions, malfunctioning equipment, and poor training and instruction.

The law does not provide workers the right to remove themselves from situations that endanger health or safety without jeopardy to their employment.